THE
LADIES
ORACLE

*You are invited to reveal your future destiny
using this unique plan, first published
in London, England in 1857.
If Queen Victoria had not already found
her Albert, she might have been one of the many
young women who consulted this work, which
'never fails to reply to any question asked'.*

The
LADIES
ORACLE

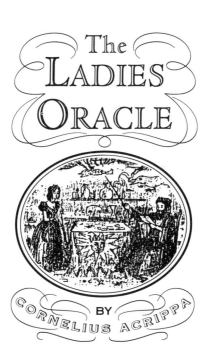

BY
CORNELIUS ACRIPPA

Copper Beech Publishing

This edition published in Great Britain 1994 by
Copper Beech Publishing Ltd
This edition © Copyright Copper Beech
Publishing Ltd.

ISBN 1-898617-00-7

A CIP catalogue record for this book is available
from the British Library.

Copper Beech Publishing Ltd
P O Box 159, East Grinstead,
Sussex, RH19 4FS England

QUESTIONS

5. Shall I soon be courted?
6. The gentleman that I am so glad to see, does he think of me?
7. Am I still thought a child?
8. Is his heart as affectionate as mine?
9. What must I do to please him?
10. Ought I to answer the first letter?
11. What will happen if I go to the appointed meeting?
12. Ought I to grant that which he asks so ardently?
13. Will my husband be young?
14. How many husbands shall I have?
15. How many lovers shall I have?
16. The one I love, what does he really think of me?
17. Ought I to believe the tender vows that are breathed to me?
18. The person that I am thinking of, does he love me?
19. The person that I am thinking of, does he think that I love him?
20. What ought I to do, to make him (that I love) love me?
21. Shall I marry young?
22. Shall I have many adventures?
23. Will my husband make me happy?
24. The man that I love, is he faithful to me?
25. Will my husband suspect me?
26. Ought I to break it off or yield?
27. Shall I have any children?
28. May I hope to receive a fortune?
29. The secret that I hide, will it be discovered?

30. Am I thought pretty?
31. What is generally thought of my intelligence?
32. If my fault is discovered, will it be pardoned?
33. Shall I cease to be a virgin before I marry?
34. Shall I marry the man I am now thinking about?
35. Shall I always enjoy good health?
36. Ought I to execute the project that I have formed?
37. Am I payed honestly?
38. Shall I be happy in love?
39. Shall I be happy long?
40. Shall I marry a rich man?
41. What disposition will my husband be?
42. My husband will he be handsome or ugly?
43. Will my husband have much intelligence?
44. Have I any rivals?
45. Are the praises (that are bestowed on me) sincere?
46. Shall I be happy in my enterprises?
47. What must I do, to prevent their discovering what I wish to conceal?
48. Shall I marry a man that I know?
49. How long will our variance last?
50. Will the reconcilement be favourable to me?
51. Does my husband love me as much as before my marriage?
52. Am I the first woman my husband has loved?
53. Has my husband loved any other woman as much as he loves me?
54. The person that I am thinking about, will he return soon?

55. Does my husband always tell me the truth?
56. The grief which now weighs me down, will it last long?
57. Shall I soon receive the news that I am expecting?
58. The affair that I am now occupied with, will it last long?
59. To which of the two persons that I am thinking about, ought I to give the preference?
60. Shall I receive the presents that I am expecting?
61. Shall I go on many long voyages?
62. The connection that I have formed, will it be lasting?
63. Will my position soon be changed?
64. Will my weakness bring the consequences that I dread?
65. Will they keep all the promises they made me?
66. Ought I to forgive?
67. Is the repentance sincere?
68. Shall I do well to confess all?
69. Ought I to take the first step towards a re-conciliation?
70. Does my husband believe me to be really virtuous?
71. Ought I to oppose the projects of my husband?
72. Am I menaced by trouble and grief?
73. Have I to expect any loss of money?
74. What is the person that I am thinking about doing at this moment?
75. Is any one envious of me?
76. Shall I receive any unexpected property?

77. Ought I to fear the tete-a-tete?
78. Will my reputation be always good?
79. Ought I to follow the advice that is given me?
80. What will be the result of my enterprise?
81. Shall I be loved long?
82. Will my life be peaceful or agitated?
83. Ought I to prefer the country or the town?
84. The fear that I have, has it any foundation?
85. Ought I to accept the propositions that are made me?
86. What will happen if I grant what they ask?
87. Shall I die maid, wife, or widow?
88. What profession will my husband follow?
89. The wish that I have at this moment will it be gratified?
90. Are they thinking of me, in the place I am thinking of?
91. What opinion has the world of me?
92. Will my heart be long disengaged?
93. Will my old age be passed happily?
94. When shall I cease to love?
95. Have I any enemies?
96. That which I desire, will it happen by night or by day?
97. That which I dread, will it happen by night or by day?
98. Ought I to forsake the pleasures of the world?
99. Will they regret me?
100. Have I to look forward to more sorrow than joy?

INSTRUCTIONS TO WORK
THE ORACLE

After having chosen a question from one of those on pages i,ii,iii and iv, shut your eyes and place your finger upon the Table beneath:-

★ ★	★ ★	★ ★ ★	★ ★ ★
★ ★ ★	★ ★ ★	★ ★ ★	★ ★ ★
★	★ ★ ★ ★	★ ★ ★ ★	★ ★ ★
★ ★ ★	★ ★ ★	★ ★ ★	★ ★ ★

You must now remember the sign on which you have placed your finger, and then consult the table, commencing at the eighth page, follow the line marked by the number of the question which you have chosen, will you arrive at the column which has the sign over it, and this figure will give you the number of the page where the answer may be found, by looking for the sign traced by your finger.

The following examples will fully explain it to you; supposing the person consulting the Oracle had chosen the eighteenth question, (The person I am thinking of does he love me?) and has placed her finger upon this sign ⁂ she would follow the eighteenth line at the eighth page, till she arrived at the column headed by the sign ⁂ which square would contain the number 75. She must then turn to the 75th page, line ⁂ and here would be the answer:

(He adores you and suffers, but he will take his revenge.)

If the person had touched this ∗∗∗ the table would have indicated 51, at which page, the line marked thus ★ ★ ★ would have answered as follows,

(His love is but a caprice and will soon pass away.)

Let us again suppose the chosen question was the twenty-fourth, (The man that I love is he faithful to me?) and the sign was ∗∗∗ at the twenty fourth line of the table, column would give page 57, and at the 57th page, the line marked thus ∗∗∗ would give this answer,

(He has always been so, and ever will be.)

Nothing is more easy or simple, and we have seen eminent and wise men struck with astonishment at the correctness of the Oracle, and never has a work of this kind been presented to the public in such a state of perfection, and we flatter ourselves that it will be universally admitted.

The following are unlucky days to work the Oracle: -
January 1,2,4,6,10,20,22, February 6,17,28, March 24,26, April 10, 27, 28 May 7,8, June 27, July 17, 21, August 20, 22, September 5, 30, October 6, November 3, 29, December 6, 10, 15.

It is not well to try the same question twice in one day.

Signs corresponding to answers on each Page

`* * *` / `* *`	`*` / `* *`	`* * *` / `* *`	`* * *` / `* *`	`* * *` / `* *`	`* * *` / `* * *`	`* * * *`	`*`	`*` / `* *`	`* *` / `* *`	`* *` / `* *`	`* *` / `* *`	`* * *`	`* * *`	`* *`	`* *`	Number of Questions
14	8	98	92	86	90	74	68	62	56	50	44	38	32	26	20	5
15	9	99	93	87	91	75	69	63	57	51	45	39	33	27	21	6
16	10	100	94	88	92	76	70	64	58	52	46	40	34	28	22	7
17	11	5	95	89	93	77	71	65	59	53	47	41	35	29	23	8
18	12	6	96	90	84	78	72	66	60	54	48	42	36	30	24	9
19	13	7	97	91	85	79	73	67	61	55	49	43	37	31	25	10
20	14	8	98	92	86	80	74	68	62	56	50	44	38	32	26	11
21	15	9	99	93	87	81	75	69	63	57	51	45	39	33	27	12
22	16	10	100	94	88	82	76	70	64	58	52	46	40	34	28	13
23	17	11	5	95	89	83	77	71	65	59	53	47	41	35	29	14
24	18	12	6	96	90	84	78	72	66	60	54	48	42	36	30	15
25	19	13	7	97	91	85	79	73	67	61	55	49	43	37	31	16
26	20	14	8	98	92	86	80	74	68	62	56	50	44	38	32	17
27	21	15	9	99	93	87	81	75	69	63	57	51	45	39	33	18
28	22	16	10	100	94	88	82	76	70	64	58	52	46	40	34	19
29	23	17	11	5	95	89	83	77	71	65	59	53	47	41	35	20
30	24	18	12	6	96	90	84	78	72	66	60	54	48	42	36	21
31	25	19	13	7	97	91	85	79	73	67	61	55	49	43	37	22
32	26	20	14	8	98	92	86	80	74	68	62	56	50	44	38	23

Signs corresponding to answers on each Page

Number of Questions	* *	**	* * *	***	* * *	* * *	* * *	* * *	*	****	* *	* * *	* * *	* * *	* *	* **
24	39	45	51	57	63	69	75	81	87	93	99	9	15	21	27	33
25	40	46	52	58	64	70	76	82	88	94	100	10	16	22	28	34
26	41	47	53	59	65	71	77	83	89	95	5	11	17	23	29	35
27	42	48	54	60	66	72	78	84	90	96	6	12	18	24	30	36
28	43	49	55	61	67	73	79	85	91	97	7	13	19	25	31	37
29	44	50	56	62	68	74	80	86	92	98	8	14	20	26	32	38
30	45	51	57	63	69	75	81	87	93	99	9	15	21	27	33	39
31	46	52	58	64	70	76	82	88	94	100	10	16	22	28	34	40
32	47	53	59	65	71	77	83	89	95	5	11	17	23	29	35	41
33	48	54	60	66	72	78	84	90	96	6	12	18	24	30	36	42
34	49	55	61	67	73	79	85	91	97	7	13	19	25	31	37	43
35	50	56	62	68	74	80	86	92	98	8	14	20	26	32	38	44
36	51	57	63	69	75	81	87	93	99	9	15	21	27	33	39	45
37	52	58	64	70	76	82	88	94	100	10	16	22	28	34	40	46
38	53	59	65	71	77	83	89	95	5	11	17	23	29	35	41	47
39	54	60	66	72	78	84	90	96	6	12	18	24	30	36	42	48
40	55	61	67	73	79	85	91	97	7	13	19	25	31	37	43	49
41	56	62	68	74	80	86	92	98	8	14	20	26	32	38	44	50
42	57	63	69	75	81	87	93	99	9	15	21	27	33	39	45	51
43	58	64	70	76	82	88	94	100	10	16	22	28	34	40	46	52

x

Signs corresponding to answers on each Page

Number of Questions	* *	**	* * *	***	* * *	* * *	* * *	* * *	*	*****	* * *	* * *	* * *	* * *	* ** *	* * *
44	59	65	71	77	83	89	95	5	11	17	23	29	35	41	47	53
45	60	66	72	78	84	90	96	6	12	18	24	30	36	42	48	54
46	61	67	73	79	85	91	97	7	13	19	25	31	37	43	49	55
47	62	68	74	80	86	92	98	8	14	20	26	32	38	44	50	56
48	63	69	75	81	87	93	99	9	15	21	27	33	39	45	51	57
49	64	70	76	82	88	94	100	10	16	22	28	34	40	46	52	58
50	65	71	77	83	89	95	5	11	17	23	29	35	41	47	53	59
51	66	72	78	84	90	96	6	12	18	24	30	36	42	48	54	60
52	67	73	79	85	91	97	7	13	19	25	31	37	43	49	55	61
53	68	74	80	86	92	98	8	14	20	26	32	38	44	50	56	62
54	69	75	81	87	93	99	9	15	21	27	33	39	45	51	57	63
55	70	76	82	88	94	100	10	16	22	28	34	40	46	52	58	64
56	71	77	83	89	95	5	11	17	23	29	35	41	47	53	59	65
57	72	78	84	90	96	6	12	18	24	30	36	42	48	54	60	66
58	73	79	85	91	97	7	13	19	25	31	37	43	49	55	61	67
59	74	80	86	92	98	8	14	20	26	32	38	44	50	56	62	68
60	75	81	87	93	99	9	15	21	27	33	39	45	51	57	63	69
61	76	82	88	94	100	10	16	22	28	34	40	46	52	58	64	70
62	77	83	89	95	5	11	17	23	29	35	41	47	53	59	65	71

Signs corresponding to answers on each Page

Number of Questions	`* *`	`* *`	`* * *`	`***`	`* * *`	`* * *`	`* *`	`* *`	`*`	`****`	`* *`	`* *`	`* *`	`* *`	`* *`	`* * *`
63	78	84	90	96	6	12	18	24	30	36	42	48	54	60	66	72
64	79	85	91	97	7	13	19	25	31	37	43	49	55	61	67	73
65	80	86	92	98	8	14	20	26	32	38	44	50	56	62	68	74
66	81	87	93	99	9	15	21	27	33	39	45	51	57	63	69	75
67	82	88	94	100	10	16	22	28	34	40	46	52	58	64	70	76
68	83	89	95	5	11	17	23	29	35	41	47	53	59	65	71	77
69	84	90	96	6	12	18	24	30	36	42	48	54	60	66	72	78
70	85	91	97	7	13	19	25	31	37	43	49	55	61	67	73	79
71	86	92	98	8	14	20	26	32	38	44	50	56	62	68	74	80
72	87	93	99	9	15	21	27	33	39	45	51	57	63	69	75	81
73	88	94	100	10	16	22	28	34	40	46	52	58	64	70	76	82
74	89	95	5	11	17	23	29	35	41	47	53	59	65	71	77	83
75	90	96	6	12	18	24	30	36	42	48	54	60	66	72	78	84
76	91	97	7	13	19	25	31	37	43	49	55	61	67	73	79	85
77	92	98	8	14	20	26	32	38	44	50	56	62	68	74	80	86
78	93	99	9	15	21	27	33	39	45	51	57	63	69	75	81	87
79	94	100	10	16	22	28	34	40	46	52	58	64	70	76	82	88
80	95	5	11	17	23	29	35	41	47	53	59	65	71	77	83	89
81	96	6	12	18	24	30	36	42	48	54	60	66	72	78	84	90

Signs corresponding to answers on each Page

Number of Questions	* **	* **	* **	* **	* * *	* * *	****	*	* *	* *	* *	* *	***	* * *	**	* *
82	91	85	79	73	67	61	55	49	43	37	31	25	19	13	7	97
83	92	86	80	74	68	62	56	50	44	38	32	26	20	14	8	98
84	93	87	81	75	69	63	57	51	45	39	33	27	21	15	9	99
85	94	88	82	76	70	64	58	52	46	40	34	28	22	16	10	100
86	95	89	83	77	71	65	59	53	47	41	35	29	23	17	11	5
87	96	90	84	78	72	66	60	54	48	42	36	30	24	18	12	6
88	97	91	85	79	73	67	61	55	49	43	37	31	25	19	13	7
89	98	92	86	80	74	68	62	56	50	44	38	32	26	20	14	8
90	99	93	87	81	75	69	63	57	51	45	39	33	27	21	15	9
91	100	94	88	82	76	70	64	58	52	46	40	34	28	22	16	10
92	5	95	89	83	77	71	65	59	53	47	41	35	29	23	17	11
93	6	96	90	84	78	72	66	60	54	48	42	36	30	24	18	12
94	7	97	91	85	79	73	67	61	55	49	43	37	31	25	19	13
95	8	98	92	86	80	74	68	62	56	50	44	38	32	26	20	14
96	9	99	93	87	81	75	69	63	57	51	45	39	33	27	21	15
97	10	100	94	88	82	76	70	64	58	52	46	40	34	28	22	16
98	11	5	95	89	83	77	71	65	59	53	47	41	35	29	23	17
99	12	6	96	90	84	78	72	66	60	54	48	42	36	30	24	18
100	13	7	97	91	85	79	73	67	61	55	49	43	37	31	25	19

★ ★	The result will be more agreeable, than useful.
★★	Very good, if you conduct yourself prudently.
★ ★ ★	He is waiting and sighing to return to you, but cannot.
★★★	Forgiveness will soon follow the avowal.
★ ★ ★	It ought to last for ever.
★ ★ ★ ★	As long as it has already lasted.
★ ★ ★	It will make you lose, as much as you would have gained by the disputes.
★ ★ ★	Two pretty ones, and one ugly one.
★	Yes, nothing will disturb your happiness.
★★★★	It would be foolish to hope for it.
★★ ★★	If you yield to-day, you will break it off to-morrow.
★ ★ ★	Weep less, and laugh more.
★ ★ ★ ★	You know how to obtain as many as you have vices.
★ ★ ★	It is much more affectionate than yours.
★ ★★ ★	It is time that you thought of repentance.
★ ★★ ★	Yet, one or two days more.

★ ★	Widow, for the second time.
★★	Nothing is lasting, and love less than all other things.
★ ★ ★	No, but your fortune will make you envied by many.
★★★	If you do so once, you will be expected to continue to do so.
★ ★ ★	Yes, if you know how to conduct yourself.
★ ★ ★	If it ever arrives, it will be before the end of three days.
★ ★ ★	It is because he loves you more, that he tries to show it less.
★ ★ ★	Not a word was meant that was said to you.
★	As long as you know how to please.
★★★★	You love pleasure too much, to wait for marriage.
★★ ★★	As much as you had before you consulted the Oracle.
★ ★ ★ ★	Very young, but not young enough to please you.
★ ★ ★ ★	You will have thirty at the least.
★ ★ ★	Let him see that you love him, and leave the rest to chance.
★ ★★	With a pretended regret and tears of decorum.
★ ★ ★ ★★ ★	Your old age will pass as pleasantly as your youth.

★ ★	Not a lucrative one.
★★	Peaceful if you are wise, agitated if you cease to be so.
★ ★ ★	You may reckon upon it, if you wish to die of hunger.
★★★	Yes, most firmly.
★ ★ ★	You will be more happy than wise.
★ ★ ★	You must not expect it at present.
★ ★ ★	You make the twenty-fifth.
★ ★ ★	Yes, as everything comes to those who have patience.
★	The gold mine has not been discovered for you.
★★★★	Yes, as soon as you like, but alas I fear too soon.
★★ ★★	Yes, but you will not know how to enjoy it.
★ ★ ★	The first will effectually prevent your looking for others.
★ ★ ★ ★	That you are a pearl.
★ ★ ★	First letters generally cause tears.
★ ★★ ★	You have nothing more to fear, but from trifles.
★ ★★ ★	When folly gives place to wisdom.

★ ★	That is impossible.
★★	Stay where you are comfortable.
★ ★ ★	You can never dread it enough.
★★★	With all your power, as they are bad.
★ ★ ★	The half only, and that will be enough.
★ ★ ★ ★	To the one that you think most about.
★ ★ ★	He has done so, and will doubtless do so again.
★ ★ ★	Show a great deal of assurance, and despise those around you.
★	As bad as yours is good.
★★★★	Yes, even against wind and tide.
★★ ★★	It has never been a secret to any one.
★ ★ ★ ★ ★	Yes, if you know how to content yourself with a little.
★ ★ ★ ★ ★	It is safer to doubt them.
★ ★ ★ ★	That it will be followed by many more.
★ ★★ ★	That should never arrive.
★ ★★ ★	Where is the simpleton that would thus lose his time.

★ ★	They do not feel interested in you, or your affairs.
★★	There is no danger but in your own fear.
★ ★ ★	Perhaps for a long time but not for ever.
★★★	It will not arrive for some time.
★ ★ ★	Follow the advice of your real friends.
★ ★ ★	Presents to entrap the young, always come too quickly.
★ ★ ★	He has not yet thought of returning.
★ ★ ★	You will have to chose between a known and an unknown one.
★	He will appear handsome to you while listening to him.
★★★★	It is a ruinous and dangerous project.
★★ ★★	As beautiful as an angel without wings.
★ ★ ★ ★	Fidelity is a quality that you have made him lose.
★ ★ ★ ★	He adored you yesterday, he loves you to-day, to-morrow.....
★ ★ ★ ★	He is not as impatient as you think, to obtain it.
★ ★★ ★	Moderately, he is a man that never acts rashly.
★ ★★ ★	After dinner.

★ ★	What you merit.
★★	Refuse them without hesitation.
★ ★ ★	Make them the guide of your conduct.
★★★	A merchant does not always gain.
★ ★ ★	More sincere than you merit.
★ ★ ★ ★	Do not forget that the longest are not always the best. Sometimes, when he fears that you will guess it.
★ ★ ★	You are expected to take the first step.
★	Happily much less than you.
★★★★	You do not merit it, and you know it well.
★★ ★★	They seldom think of absent friends.
★ ★ ★	Never, unless you oblige him to.
★ ★ ★	He believes that you love another better than him.
★ ★ ★	He will be middle-aged and not at all learned.
★ ★★ ★	They think you a child that has nothing more to learn.
★ ★★ ★	At mid-day, in the shade.

★ ★★	It is already lost.
★★	That you will not be able to refuse anything after it.
★ ★ ★	You should not take the slightest notice of them.
★★★	The person curses the destiny that keeps him from you.
★ ★ ★	Frankness never injured any one.
★ ★ ★	That will absolutely depend on your conduct.
★ ★ ★	It ought to last longer than it really will.
★ ★ ★	It will be a great calamity for you.
★	Yes, one that you think your friend.
★★★★	Sometimes, in the night.
★★ ★★	You have nothing to expect, but to be despised.
★ ★ ★ ★	As the proverb says, it is better to bend than break.
★ ★ ★ ★	Endeavour to lose the quality that you have too much of.
★ ★ ★ ★	As many as your first husband will have had wives.
★ ★★ ★	The poor boy does not yet know whether he has one.
★ ★★ ★	In a twelvemonth at the latest.

★ ★	More than you have merited.
★★	Widow, if you are not married before you are twenty.
★ ★ ★	As many as you have the art to deceive.
★★★	Yes, but they are not powerful.
★ ★ ★	Be upon your guard, and let them come to you.
★ ★ ★	It will change if you change it, not else.
★ ★ ★	Like all good news it will come quickly.
★ ★ ★	No, because you are not amiable.
★	Yes, for the person who praised you, is no flatterer.
★★★★	The more lively your joy, the sooner it will terminate.
★★ ★★	No, as you will be married sooner than you expect.
★ ★ ★	Several, who will make you very happy.
★ ★ ★ ★	You will have the opportunity, but you will refuse.
★ ★ ★ ★	When you have counted ten, you will have still to count.
★ ★★ ★	You must be less giddy and more sensible.
★ ★★ ★	They will never regret you enough.

$\begin{matrix}\star\\\star\end{matrix}$	When you cease to live.
$\star\star$	A lucrative profession.
$\begin{matrix}\star\\\star\\\star\end{matrix}$	Much more peaceful than it has been up to the present time.
$\star\star\star$	You will inherit nothing but what your industry procures you.
$\begin{matrix}\star\\\star\\\star\end{matrix}$	He believes nothing but the truth.
$\begin{matrix}\star\\\star\\\star\end{matrix}$	Be assured that the danger is passed.
$\begin{matrix}\star\\\star\ \ \star\end{matrix}$	It would be better for you if it never ended.
$\begin{matrix}\star\ \ \star\\\star\end{matrix}$	He has only loved six fair ones and nine dark ones.
$\star$	Do not build upon the success of them.
$\star\star\star\star$	His fortune will be as shallow as his love.
$\begin{matrix}\star\star\\\star\star\end{matrix}$	You must be, as you are already engaged.
$\begin{matrix}\star\\\star\\\star\ \ \star\end{matrix}$	Enough to be happy with.
$\begin{matrix}\star\ \ \star\\\star\\\star\end{matrix}$	Women like you, have always too many or too few.
$\begin{matrix}\star\\\star\ \ \star\\\star\end{matrix}$	That you can be either an angel or a demon.
$\begin{matrix}\star\\\star\star\\\star\end{matrix}$	Answer it when you may, it will be too soon for your happiness.
$\begin{matrix}\star\\\star\star\ \ \star\end{matrix}$	The fortunate hour will soon come for you.

★ ★	Even an insect has many.
★★	At the time you least expect it.
★ ★ ★	To live in the country you would require more simplicity than you have at present.
★★★	Do not trust yourself, it is dangerous.
★ ★ ★	Yes, when he wishes to exercise authority over you.
★ ★ ★	Yes, if you keep those, which they made you promise.
★ ★ ★	To the one that appears in the least hurry.
★ ★ ★	He could not say no, without telling a lie.
★	Before everything else, follow the dictates of your heart.
★★★★	It will change from bad to worse.
★★ ★★	The Doctors will tell you No, the Oracle tells you Yes.
★ ★ ★ ★	Be discreet and fear nothing.
★ ★ ★ ★ ★	He will not trouble himself about you, more than the year forty.
★ ★ ★	No, they are not meant.
★ ★★ ★	That you lose a little, and gain a great deal.
★ ★★ ★ ★	When you have more sense.

★ ★	If you are foolish in the day, if you are wise in the night.
★★	A little occasionally.
★ ★ ★	You must be foolish to fear that.
★★★	You are too foolish to know how to retain it.
★ ★ ★	If you have, they will be of your own making.
★ ★ ★	Do not be too hasty about it.
★ ★ ★	You will lose nothing by waiting.
★ ★ ★	He is already on the road, but is coming slowly.
★	He knows you, but you do not know him.
★★★★	Neither one or the other.
★★ ★★	It is too late.
★ ★ ★ ★	Too much so, sometimes.
★ ★ ★ ★ ★	Men are never faithful to those they have ceased to love.
★ ★ ★ ★ ★	He loves you, but differently from what you wish him to.
★ ★★	If you do not grant it, you will allow him to take it.
★ ★★ ★	Give him a little encouragement, and he will do more than think.

★ ★	You ought never to be.
★★	They think you better than you really are.
★ ★ ★	Yes, because you have nothing to risk.
★★★	Consult your good sense before everything.
★ ★ ★	You have lost more than you will ever lose again.
★ 　★ ★	It is an actor's repentance, laughing with one eye and crying with the other.
★ ★ ★	Remember that a rolling stone gathers no moss.
★ ★ ★	Always the truth, therefore believe it.
★	Till the end of the moon.
★★★★	Much more than you will ever have.
★★ ★★	They return you more than you give.
★ ★ ★	They excuse your not having much, but cannot excuse your pretension.
★ ★ ★	Perhaps, but he will not say anything.
★ ★ ★ ★	He believes more in your love than in your wisdom.
★ ★★ ★	He will be a little past the middle age.
★★ ★ ★	They only require to see you, to judge for themselves.

★ ★ ★	Sometime, after to-day.
★★	But a very short time.
★ ★ ★	Very little good but much evil will follow.
★★★	Folly cannot produce good effects.
★ ★ ★	He is now holding a conversation with a very pretty woman.
★ ★ ★	Avow it, if you have the courage.
★ ★ ★	You cannot break it off too soon.
★ ★ ★	By the next new moon all will have passed away.
★	Very favourable, if you know how to act.
★★★★	That should not trouble you.
★★ ★★	Yes, as happy as you are young and pretty.
★ ★ ★ ★	They have already pardoned you too much.
★ ★ ★ ★	If you do not yield to-day, you will to-morrow.
★ ★ ★ ★	Obtain a fortune, there is no surer method of being beloved.
★ ★★	Four, and you will like neither of them.
★ ★★ ★	No, but it will gradually become so.

★ ★	They will forget you too soon for that.
★★	Yes, if you know how to be content with a little.
★ ★ ★	Maid, if you continue so another year.
★★★	Until you are well known.
★ ★ ★	Do not be curious yourself and you will have nothing to fear.
★ ★ ★	Be contented to make the second.
★ ★ ★	You will have to wait long for the change.
★ ★ ★	He will arrive when you are not expecting him.
★	That depends on the time and his temper.
★★★★	They are not to be depended on.
★★ ★★	Happiness will make you long visits after short absences.
★ ★ ★	The two things will be accomplished the same day.
★ ★ ★ ★	Three, and they will be to be pitied if they are like their mother.
★ ★ ★	You will be married before you have attained a reasonable age.
★ ★★ ★	You appear in the humour to add four more to your hundred.
★★ ★ ★	Nothing, for he loves you as much as it is possible to love.

★ ★	As much of one as the other.
★★	After you have passed your sixtieth year.
★ ★ ★	An excessively lucrative and honourable one.
★★★	Peace will follow agitation.
★ ★ ★	Never depend upon yourself.
★ ★ ★	He regards your virtue as the most splended jewel of his crown.
★ ★ ★	It cannot have any.
★ ★ ★	Do not trouble yourself so much about it, wait patiently.
★	Upon this point I think you are equal.
★★★★	Rarely, perhaps once in ten times.
★★ ★★	Small fortune and little intellect.
★ ★ ★ ★	If you marry him you will repent it.
★ ★ ★ ★	Yes, if you do not sacrifice usefulness to agreeableness.
★ ★ ★ ★	A wise woman has always too many.
★ ★★ ★	That you have more neatness than grace, and more grace than love.
★ ★★ ★	Reply and say, Adieu, Casket; the jewel that thou wantest is not in my power to give.

* * *	Much too soon for your happiness.
**	Those which you have are to be feared.
* * *	You will sigh a long time for it.
***	The town alone suits you.
* * *	It promises you nothing but pleasure.
* * *	You are already too much opposed to them.
* * *	You must be mad to believe it.
* * *	To the one that knows your secret.
*	Yes, but it has not been so long.
****	Defy all those around you.
** **	He will drink like a fish.
* * * *	Doctors will not ruin you.
* * * * *	No, if you persuade yourself not to talk so much at night.
* * *	Every where and at all times and places.
* ** *	The promises may be good, but a security would be better.
* ** *	Nothing that can in any wise astonish you.

★ ★	He thinks more about you by night than by day.
★★	By day and by night.
★ ★ ★	Yes, but it will be very badly arranged.
★★★	Rest peaceably, and all will go well.
★ ★ ★	It is absolutely impossible.
★ ★ ★	Frequent, but not lasting sorrow.
★ ★ ★	Make them wait for it, but grant it in the end.
★ ★ ★	That will depend upon what you do to merit them.
★	He will very soon return.
★★★★	You will marry a former lover.
★★ ★★	He will be quite handsome enough for you.
★ ★ ★	Whenever you do it, it will be done too soon.
★ ★ ★ ★	You are generally thought to have been pretty.
★ ★ ★ ★	He says Yes, the Oracle says No.
★ ★★ ★	He loves you, and you are his first love.
★ ★★ ★	That will be the way to make him ungrateful.

★ ★	Every one knows that you have ceased to be one.
★★	That which you fear, you should desire ardently.
★ ★ ★	Neither good or bad.
★★★	You can without danger.
★ ★ ★	Yes, but not blindfold.
★ ★ ★	Loss of money is better than loss of friends.
★ ★ ★	Has sincerity anything to do with it.
★ ★ ★	Only one, and that will cost you a great deal.
★	He has never been in the habit of telling lies.
★★★★	Until the first fine day in May.
★★ ★★	He will have enough to eat up his wealth.
★ ★ ★ ★	They do not know enough of you.
★ ★ ★ ★	That you would do well to take care of what you have.
★ ★ ★	His suspicions will be like a cloud, they soon pass away.
★ ★★ ★	He believes you to be a coquette, and he knows they never love any one.
★ ★★ ★	He will be younger than you.

★ ★	It is much more affectionate, and he is more generous than you.
★★	Yes, if you wish them to regret you.
★ ★ ★	You are very impatient to throw yourself away.
★★★	Neither good or bad will result from it.
★ ★ ★	It is not conducted well enough to succeed.
★ ★ ★	He is trying to find out how he can best deceive you.
★ ★ ★	It will be of no consequence, you can do as you feel inclined.
★ ★ ★ ★	It will last half the time that it has already lasted.
★	If you had acted reasonably, it would have been ended.
★★★★	You will not profit much by it.
★★ ★★	You will soon have some, if you do not give way to bad temper.
★ ★ ★	Yes, until you are wrinkled.
★ ★ ★ ★	They will forgive you, but you will soon begin again.
★ ★ ★ ★	Remember that women are to obey.
★ ★★ ★	Do not reproach him, when he is wrong.
★ ★★ ★	Three, if you are married in three weeks.

★ ★	Grant him all that he asks.
★★	Never.
★ ★ ★	It will be passed in opulence.
★★★	Widow, if you are one now.
★ ★ ★	That it will not last long, but it will soon begin again.
★ ★ ★	You have many among persons you think friends.
★ ★ ★	That would really be a clergyman's step.
★ ★ ★	It will become more brilliant, but not better.
★	Sooner than you ought to for your future happiness.
★★★★	Sometimes more and sometimes less.
★★ ★★	Sincere and merited.
★ ★ ★ ★	Happiness is too fragile a thing to last long.
★ ★ ★	How could you doubt such a thing.
★ ★ ★	Only one who will be as amiable as yourself.
★ ★★ ★	Young girls like you will marry, they will not be kept from it.
★ ★★ ★	A great many, but those that have so many generally choose the worst.

★ ★	When you are asked a question like that, the affair is half settled.
★★	Little pleasure and little grief.
★ ★ ★	Never.
★★★	Not any.
★ ★ ★	If you agitate the ocean you must expect a storm.
★ ★ ★	If you count upon it you are lost.
★ ★ ★	He loves but you and always relies upon you.
★ ★ ★	Not those which you dread, but others more to be feared.
★	Some weighty obstacles delay the solution.
★★★★	If he has not done better than you, he has not done worse.
★★ ★★	Always in spite of good sense and reason.
★ ★ ★ ★	Too much for his honour and yours also.
★ ★ ★ ★	If he leaves you, adieu to happiness.
★ ★ ★ ★	Yes, if you know how to keep a pear against you if you are thirsty.
★ ★★ ★	They are preparing for you, and you will not be able to resist them.
★ ★★ ★	That you will soon deceive him, and he is right.

★ ★	What have you to fear, as you have nothing to lose.
★★	You are in too great a hurry.
★ ★ ★	You have none at present.
★★★	Never completely.
★ ★ ★	You are not wise enough to renounce the pleasures of the town.
★ ★ ★ ★	If you are married, Yes; if not, No.
★ ★ ★	Give him advice, but do not tease him.
★ ★ ★	With difficulty, but they will keep them.
★	To the youngest if he is thirty years of age.
★★★★	No, and that will never happen.
★★ ★★	Trust to no one but God and yourself.
★ ★ ★ ★	Honest, upright, never thinking ill of any one.
★ ★ ★ ★	You will have good health and will live long.
★ ★ ★ ★	To-morrow if not to-day.
★ ★★ ★	In the morning, at mid-day, and at midnight.
★ ★★ ★	To believe them would be to confide yourself to enemies with your hands and feet tied.

★ ★	As well to-day as to-morrow, since you must do it.
★★	He has more important things to think about.
★ ★ ★	In the night, when all cats are alive.
★★★	They are singing your praises.
★ ★ ★	It has not the slightest foundation.
★ ★ ★	It will not last as long as it has lasted.
★ ★ ★	The worst is passed.
★ ★ ★	Yes, but make them guarantee for the future.
★	The longer you wait the more valuable they will be.
★★★★	Sooner than you wish.
★★ ★★	You will either marry your first or your last lover.
★ ★ ★ ★	Much handsomer than those which preceded him.
★ ★ ★ ★	The results are uncertain.
★ ★ ★ ★	It was thought that you would have been prettier.
★ ★★ ★	Ask him this, and believe what he tells you.
★ ★★ ★	Slightly, moderately, when his occupations allow him.

★ ★ ★	The one destined for you is not yet born.
★★	Yes, but as a child, capable of drawing others after you.
★ ★ ★	In the middle of the night.
★★★	A detestable opinion.
★ ★ ★	They hide a snare for you.
★ ★ ★	Take care: they wish to drive you into their trap.
★ ★ ★	You have to lose or gain.
★ ★ ★	You may believe it in all security.
★	Several by land and by sea.
★★★★	He is a great boaster.
★★ ★★	If it finishes to-night it will begin again to-morrow.
★ ★ ★	He will not have much, and will not know how to use that.
★ ★ ★ ★	Sincere and unchanging.
★ ★ ★	That it is a wanton flame which will soon extinguish itself.
★ ★★ ★	Suspicions seldom enter into a noble heart.
★ ★★ ★	Yes, but he will not believe it long.

★ ★	Only one, and that will be one too much.
★★	He has only the place where his heart once was.
★ ★ ★	In ten or twelve years.
★★★	Yes, if you are wise.
★ ★ ★	When peas are sown, beans are not expected to grow up.
★ ★ ★	It will be happily terminated.
★ ★ ★	He is thinking seriously and gravely.
★ ★ ★	Rather to-day than to-morrow.
★	It will be longer than happy.
★★★★	The sharper the pain, the shorter the duration.
★★ ★★	If you are too easy, you will repent of it.
★ ★ ★	You will never have more than rivals of a day.
★ ★ ★ ★	You will find more pain than pleasure.
★ ★ ★	Yes, they cannot do otherwise.
★ ★★ ★	Break it off if possible, but yield if you dare.
★ ★★ ★	If you do not trouble about him, he will think more of you.

★ ★	Can the stars of the sky or the sand of the sea shore be counted?
★★	You must try to become better than you are.
★ ★ ★	They will weep after you for a long time.
★★★	It ought not to be, but nevertheless it will be.
★ ★ ★	You will be the same at your death that you are now.
★ ★ ★	Always, if you do not change.
★ ★ ★	Approaching events will disembarrass you of them.
★ ★ ★	It will not take place except you do.
★	Yes, and you will not be happier for it.
★★★★	You have need of much patience.
★★ ★★	Do you think that flies are preserved in vinegar?
★ ★ ★	Words light as air, which may be blown by every breeze.
★ ★ ★ ★	Nothing is lasting, much less happiness.
★ ★ ★	Who in the world do you think would have any thing to do with you?
★ ★★ ★	Yes, when you have found what you have not now.
★ ★★ ★	Have patience for you must wait a long time.

★ ★	He finds you charming...Love is blind.
★★	Words fly away; but writing always remains.
★ ★ ★	Joy will always follow grief.
★★★	When your hair becomes grey.
★ ★ ★	Several, and not one good one.
★ ★ ★	The agitation will be of short duration.
★ ★ ★	Industry is the best fortune.
★ ★ ★	He begins to suspect the truth.
★	Yes, but they will pardon you.
★★★★	There are yet many obstacles to overcome.
★★ ★★	You had enough experience to perceive it.
★ ★ ★	You will have two reverses for each success.
★ ★ ★ ★	You will only marry him for his money.
★ ★ ★ ★	Marry, if you can.
★ ★★ ★	No, if your taste does not change.
★ ★★ ★	You will have so many that you will be disgusted.

★ ★	To promise and to perform are two things.
★★	You will only have one more fault to reproach yourself with.
★ ★ ★	It would be necessary to change your character a little for this.
★★★	You have had some, but you have none at present.
★ ★ ★	Not without much difficulty.
★ ★ ★	The country agrees with your health, but the town with your taste.
★ ★ ★	The happiest moments of your life will be passed there.
★ ★ ★	It is the way to disturb the peace of your household.
★	They will only be too happy to do so.
★★★★	To the one that appears the most patient.
★★ ★★	A man never really loves but once.
★ ★ ★ ★	Fear treason with all your might.
★ ★ ★ ★	Ardent, passionate, a perfect libertine.
★ ★ ★ ★	Yes, if you keep your feet warm, head cool, and body open.
★ ★★ ★	Sooner or later it must arrive.
★ ★★ ★	You will be more happy than wise with him.

★ ★	He is not fool enough for that.
★★	You must, for you do not know the way to say No.
★ ★ ★	He never has, does not, and never will.
★★★	By day or by night, the results will be the same.
★ ★ ★	They think a great deal about you.
★ ★ ★	You have absolutely nothing to fear.
★ ★ ★	It is already lost.
★ ★ ★	Many trials await you, but resign yourself.
★	Pardon them, and in eight days they will begin again.
★★★★	You will be wrong to think about them.
★★ ★★	Soon enough to vex you very much.
★ ★ ★ ★	Your future husband, is an old friend of the family.
★ ★ ★ ★	Morally handsome, but physically ugly.
★ ★ ★ ★	It ought to be already executed.
★ ★★	Yes, but they do not love you more.
★ ★★ ★	He is not now, but he may become so.

★ ★	Fools alone believe in impossibilities.
★★	He will neither have teeth, or hair and will be gouty.
★ ★ ★	Every one knows that you do not wish to be thought one.
★★★	In sunshine.
★ ★ ★	They think you are envious.
★ ★ ★	Yes, if they please you.
★ ★ ★	Follow them, as they are good.
★ ★ ★	You ought to know how to sacrifice a little to prevent a great loss.
★	Much less than he appears to have.
★★★★	When one is all right, they should learn to keep so.
★★ ★★	Yes, when he neither says Yes or No.
★ ★ ★	Say but one word and it will instantly stop.
★ ★ ★	Just enough to be able to manage himself.
★ ★ ★	You love less than you are loved.
★ ★★ ★	That it is not much good to yourself or any one else.
★ ★★ ★	He will always have too much self-esteem to think that you deceive him.

★ ★	Nothing, as he already adores you.
★★	As many as you have had lovers.
★ ★ ★	It is as affectionate, but less ardent and more faithful.
★★★	Why renounce that which forms your happiness.
★ ★ ★	It will not be so to-morrow.
★ ★ ★	That you will soon repent of it.
★ ★ ★	You will be wrong to count upon its success.
★ ★ ★	He is committing various follies.
★	Wait until the tempest calms.
★★★★	It will have more charm than duration.
★★ ★★	You have not much more to suffer.
★ ★ ★ ★	It will be the greatest misfortune of your life.
★ ★ ★	They fear you too much for that.
★ ★ ★ ★	Love will be a Paradise for you.
★ ★★ ★	It is prudent not to reckon upon it.
★ ★★ ★	Break it off, to have the pleasures of a reconciliation.

★ ★	It will always arrive too soon.
★★	As many as you find to deceive.
★ ★ ★	You must be wise, devoted, and amiable.
★★★	Very much.
★ ★ ★	Very happy.
★ ★ ★	You cannot die a maid.
★ ★ ★	As much as you love yourself.
★ ★ ★	You will soon have many.
★	The words (I am wrong) ought not to keep you silent.
★★★★	It will change sooner or later.
★★ ★★	Hope and wait patiently.
★ ★ ★	He would love you now, had you continued to be amiable.
★ ★ ★	Sincere, but little merited.
★ ★ ★	You are too inconstant to be always happy.
★ ★★ ★	A pretty woman can appear to be any thing she likes.
★ ★★ ★	You will have some sooner or later.

★ ★	A little by day, and very much by night.
★★	He thinks a little bad, but very much good.
★ ★ ★	Yes, if you are decided to refuse nothing.
★★★	More grief than joy.
★ ★ ★	In ten years, if not before.
★ ★ ★ ★	He will be good for nothing.
★ ★ ★	Very agitated, but it will be your own fault.
★ ★ ★	Yes, but it is very distant.
★	He did believe it, but he no longer does.
★★★★	Yes, and it will be profitable to you.
★★ ★★	It will be better for your happiness if it does not terminate soon.
★ ★ ★ ★	It is because he loved so much, that he should be pardoned.
★ ★ ★ ★	You will be successful twice for every reverse.
★ ★ ★ ★	You will believe him rich, but he will be poor.
★ ★★	Alas, a little too late.
★ ★★ ★	You will arrive at fortune by the road of pleasure.

★ ★	Yes, every other day.
★★	In a similar case, seeing is believing.
★ ★ ★	By no means accept it you will only be laughed at.
★★★	What simpleton would thus lose his time.
★ ★ ★	You have not amongst the gentlemen.
★ ★ ★	Yes, in a short time.
★ ★ ★	The country would be very dull for you.
★ ★ ★	Those that do not wish to do wrong should not fear.
★	Slowly as though you were not doing so.
★★★★	If they do not keep them it will be your fault.
★★ ★★	To-day to one, and to-morrow to the other.
★ ★ ★ ★ ★	He has loved all the ladies in the same way.
★ ★ ★ ★ ★	Do not trouble yourself as you do about the first word.
★ ★ ★ ★	False, quarrelsome, and dissipated.
★ ★★ ★	Always without a doctor, never with one.
★ ★ ★★ ★ ★	Yes, but more good than bad will result.

★ ★	Sometimes for two days entire.
★★	A little, as he has loved a thousand others.
★ ★ ★	You know very well that you will not make him a very beautiful present.
★★★	Sometimes, when he has nothing better to do.
★ ★ ★	During the day, if in summer.
★ ★ ★	They think more of themselves than you.
★ ★ ★	You should desire what you now fear.
★ ★ ★	It will soon be reduced to its just value.
★	You will have more than you have had.
★★★★	Yes, for the repentance is sincere.
★★ ★★	They have changed their minds on this point.
★ ★ ★ ★	Too late for him, too soon for you.
★ ★ ★ ★	The one destined for you, is not yet breeched.
★ ★ ★ ★	Physically handsome, morally ugly.
★ ★★ ★	You must walk uprightly, any thing else would be fatal.
★ ★★ ★	Ugly and foolish, and that is not all.

★ ★	He will never know more than half the truth.
★★	He knows that you wish for nothing better than his love.
★ ★ ★	Young and handsome.
★★★	They take you for what you are.
★ ★ ★	Once by night, and twice by day.
★ ★ ★	You are thought to be very giddy.
★ ★ ★	No, if you have not resolution.
★ ★ ★	You will not know how to follow better ones.
★	You will be very lucky, if you lose nothing but money.
★★★★	Sincerity does not inspire such fine phrases.
★★ ★★	A very short sentimental voyage.
★ ★ ★ ★	He would sooner tear out his tongue.
★ ★ ★ ★	Until you change your conduct.
★ ★ ★ ★	An agreeable mind, and well cultivated.
★ ★★ ★	You have no sincerity yourself.
★ ★★ ★	That you can make better use of it.

★ ★	To break is difficult, but to yield is very easy.
★★	A very difficult thing; be discreet.
★ ★ ★	You will have a dozen, and each time will be master, but the thirteenth will be your master.
★★★	He will try to find out first whether you have an affectionate heart.
★ ★ ★	Wait till you are older.
★ ★ ★	Yes, it will be the same in three months as it is to-day.
★ ★ ★	The first concession always calls for others.
★ ★ ★	You will succeed, but with much difficulty.
★	He is thinking of an approaching separation.
★★★★	It is always best to tell all.
★★ ★★	It will have more duration than charm.
★ ★ ★ ★ ★	Time alone can calm it.
★ ★ ★ ★ ★	It will not cost you much, nor will it bring you much.
★ ★ ★ ★ ★	A prettier one than you and more clever.
★ ★★ ★	Yes, if you know how to be contented with a little.
★ ★★ ★	Yes, but after much punishment.

★ ★ ★	A boy and a girl.
★★	The later the better.
★ ★ ★	As many as you wish, and you with for a great many.
★★★	Be loving, and show it unceasingly.
★ ★ ★	They only regret those they really love.
★ ★ ★	Enough to make you regret life.
★ ★ ★	You will die before your first husband.
★ ★ ★	Until you are wrinkled.
★	One is always envied by those that are inferior.
★★★★	Neither the first or the last.
★★ ★★	It will change in the course of the year.
★ ★ ★ ★	One day more will pass before he sets out.
★ ★ ★ ★	He loved you before, but now he adores you.
★ ★ ★ ★ ★	They wished to blind you by their praises.
★ ★★ ★	That will depend upon yourself.
★ ★★ ★	Virgin or not, you will be adored.

★ ★	You will be as poor as Job, but not as patient.
★★	Yes, but they will end badly.
★ ★ ★	He is too loving to think about anything but loving you.
★★★	Speak but little and write still less.
★ ★ ★	Harmless joy and no sorrow.
★ ★ ★	Very soon.
★ ★ ★	You will always want him too much to allow him to think of a profession.
★ ★ ★	More peaceful than most people would have thought.
★	You will receive when you will not want it.
★★★★	He knows you very well.
★★ ★★	No.
★ ★ ★ ★	Before the end of the next moon.
★ ★ ★	Yes, for he never loved before he loved you.
★ ★ ★ ★	Yes, if you change your conduct.
★ ★★ ★	Your good fortune will soon pass away.
★ ★★ ★	Yes, but it will be a forced marriage.

★ ★	It has been known by everybody for a long time.
★★	Not as much as you merit.
★ ★ ★	Similar promises are generally forgotten like a dream.
★★★	First pleasure, then grief.
★ ★ ★	You will be wrinkled before that arrives.
★ ★ ★ ★	Defy the women that are around you.
★ ★ ★	If it is not soon, it will never be.
★ ★ ★	The town alone suits you.
★	You should fear the consequences.
★★★★	His projects are wise, you must be mad.
★★ ★★	They would like to dispense with them, but cannot.
★ ★ ★ ★	Do not choose at all, keep them both.
★ ★ ★ ★	He will never love you as much as he has loved others.
★ ★ ★ ★	Always hold your tongue, wherever you may be.
★ ★★ ★	He will be a Misanthrophe.
★ ★★ ★	Your health depends upon your own inclination.

★ ★	You would have to change your countenance to do that.
★★	He gives you the value of your money.
★ ★ ★	Yes, like you love him.
★★★	Grant it, my child, it will be rendered to you again.
★ ★ ★	He thinks too much, for he will repent of it.
★ ★ ★	The night, if in winter.
★ ★ ★	They are only making fun of you.
★ ★ ★	Do what is right, and fear nothing.
★	You may deceive for a long time, but not for ever.
★★★★	Childish sorrow that will soon be dissipated.
★★ ★★	He is incorrigible.
★ ★ ★ ★	They are preparing them for you to admire.
★ ★ ★ ★	Too soon for him, too late for you.
★ ★ ★ ★	You will marry the man that is now courting you.
★ ★★ ★	As handsome as you can wish.
★ ★★ ★	Without hesitating an instant.

★ ★	That is more brilliant than solid.
★★	You can make him believe all that you like.
★ ★ ★	He did believe, but he does not now.
★★★	He carried a sword before you were born.
★ ★ ★	They would more likely wish you really were one.
★ ★ ★	In the night, happily for you.
★ ★ ★	They all agree in saying that you are not very amiable.
★ ★ ★	No harm can possibly result from it.
★	Your heart will always be your best guide.
★★★★	That which you will lose will not be worth looking after.
★★ ★★	No, it is only a pretence.
★ ★ ★ ★	You are too changeable to remain long where you are.
★ ★ ★ ★	He respects truth but never speaks it.
★ ★ ★ ★	Until you have merited forgiveness.
★ ★★ ★	You will never before have met with such an intellectual man.
★ ★★ ★	Yes, they cheat you, the same as you cheat them.

★ ★ ★	It may be forgiven, but cannot be forgotten.
★★	If I advise you to break it off, you will not.
★ ★ ★	Be tolerant, and know how to pardon.
★★★	An old one and a young one; but you will not be satisfied with either.
★ ★ ★	It is like yours, very sensitive but not very constant.
★ ★ ★	You ought to have already renounced it.
★ ★ ★	It has been so more than it will ever be again.
★ ★ ★	That you will enter into a road where you will find it impossible to stop.
★	You will be poorer after than before.
★★★★	He is not doing anything, and is not thinking about you.
★★ ★★	To sin and to confess, is to be half forgiven.
★ ★ ★	You are not constant enough for that.
★ ★ ★ ★	You are not a woman to die of grief.
★ ★ ★ ★	I should not like to have what you will gain.
★ ★★ ★	You will soon be surrounded by them.
★ ★★ ★	Never; it is your destiny.

★ ★	More than ten years before.
★★	Yes, that is certain.
★ ★ ★	Yes, as there will be an urgency.
★★★	A complete dozen, and a very little one to make thirteen. You should follow all their counsels blindfold.
★ ★ ★	They will appear to do so.
★ ★ ★	As much as to youthfulness.
★ ★ ★	As much as to youthfulness.
★ ★ ★	You will have been all these before your death.
★	Yes, until you are grey headed.
★★★★	Why should that trouble you, the envious one only suffers.
★★ ★★	If you do it, you will repent of it.
★ ★ ★ ★	Yes, very often like your temper.
★ ★ ★ ★	He will be prevented by an unforseen event.
★ ★ ★ ★	Much less, but he will love you more by and by.
★ ★★ ★	It was only a bait thrown out to your vanity.
★ ★★ ★	Yes, but not always in the same manner.

★ ★	Yes, and several others.
★★	Hope so, for to hope is to enjoy.
★ ★ ★	You will look for more than you will find.
★★★	Oysters live but they do not think.
★ ★ ★	Yes, as it is dangerous.
★ ★ ★	You have suffered enough, you should now rejoice.
★ ★ ★	To-day .... or to-morrow.
★ ★ ★	A dangerous profession.
★	A calm always follows a storm.
★★★★	Neither hope or fear.
★★ ★★	He does not know one of your actions.
★ ★ ★ ★	You merit them but you will not have them.
★ ★ ★ ★	If it is not in three days, it will be in three months.
★ ★ ★ ★	He has had several to pass the time away.
★ ★★ ★	You will only succeed in minor things.
★ ★★ ★	Great fortune, little heart, and very little brains.

★ ★	You cannot expect good health without wisdom.
★★	It is a theatrical secret everybody knows it.
★ ★ ★	Much more than you merit him to be.
★★★	To believe without examining would be foolish.
★ ★ ★	It will not make much difference to you.
★ ★ ★	Yes, but it will only be to make fun of you.
★ ★ ★	You ought to fear but one.
★ ★ ★	Yes, and it will be the worse for you.
★	Live in the country if you wish for good health.
★★★★	Yes, and many other things.
★★ ★★	If you oppose him, you will have cause to regret it.
★ ★ ★ ★	They would retract if they could.
★ ★ ★ ★	To the youngest if you prefer pleasure to fortune.
★ ★ ★ ★ ★	The love that you inspire him with, is felt but once.
★ ★★ ★	Do not forget that your steps are watched.
★ ★★ ★	Brave, liberal and gallant.

★ ★ ★	As soon as possible.
★★	Very pretty, but not very amiable.
★ ★ ★	Yes, he cannot do otherwise.
★★★	His love is a caprice that will soon end.
★ ★ ★	Take care if you wish to retain his heart.
★ ★ ★	How can he avoid it, when he adores you.
★ ★ ★	Perhaps it will never arrive.
★ ★ ★	They are too busy to trouble themselves about you.
★	Never was fear more ridiculous.
★★★★	It will always be according to your merit.
★★ ★★	You must give way to what you cannot prevent.
★ ★ ★	If you forgive them to-day, they will laugh at you to-morrow.
★ ★ ★ ★	They have not had time to think about them.
★ ★ ★ ★	He will always come soon enough to play you tricks.
★ ★★ ★	You will marry one that often makes you sigh.
★ ★★ ★	Too handsome, for you will suffer by it.

★ ★ ★	They are making game of you.
★★	That it is the devil's intelligence.
★ ★ ★	Yes, without he is deaf or blind.
★★★	He does not trouble about it, but makes fine fun of it.
★ ★ ★	Hoary headed, white bearded, and trembling limbs.
★ ★ ★	You are not innocent enough for that.
★ ★ ★	It will often arrive, and at all hours.
★ ★ ★	They think that you commit many follies.
★	Yes, they will make no difference.
★★★★	Councillors multiply, but wisdom is scarce.
★★ ★★	There are good reasons why you should not lose anything.
★ ★ ★ ★	They do not repent more than you do.
★ ★ ★ ★	You will do so, though you will not be obliged to.
★ ★ ★ ★ ★	You would be much surprised if he did not tell stories sometimes.
★ ★★ ★	Yet another month or so.
★ ★★ ★	Enough not to ask you anything about the last.

★ ★	Those who are happy in love, do not always merit it.
★★	It can be forgiven but never forgotten.
★ ★ ★	Break it off, if you are wise, yield if you would be happy.
★★★	Do as he wishes and do not consult your own feelings.
★ ★	As many as you will have children.
★ ★ ★	He has the heart of a cock who struts on a dunghill and thinks but of himself.
★ ★ ★	Yes, for there is no good in it for you.
★ ★ ★	The longer the better.
★	That a second step will follow the first.
★★★★	It will be prompt and fruitful.
★★ ★★	He is building castles in the air.
★ ★ ★	Do not forget that there are many ways of doing things.
★ ★ ★	Scarcely was it formed when you tried to break it.
★ ★ ★	Yes, but one is not obliged to die, to learn how to suffer.
★ ★★ ★	It will give you pleasure unmixed with pain.
★ ★★ ★	You have had them, you will have them.

★ ★	A few hours in a few years.
★★	When you marry, your first children will have teeth.
★ ★ ★	Three, and they will be very handsome.
★★★	Yes, without rector or parson.
★ ★ ★	Yes, as many as you had bad thoughts last night.
★ ★ ★	Show yourself wiser than you are.
★ ★ ★	They will show you justice.
★ ★ ★	Your position will not change from here to there.
★	You will die a maid, if you are not married before thirty.
★★★★	A long time, but faintly.
★★ ★★	Yes, but they have seldom any power.
★ ★ ★ ★	It will be profitable to you to do so.
★ ★ ★ ★	If it is not changed in a month, it will never change.
★ ★ ★ ★	They are trying to send it to you.
★ ★★ ★	The love before and after marriage is not to be compared.
★ ★★ ★	No, the one that made them was blind.

★ ★	Neither rich or poor.
★★	He will not marry you.
★ ★ ★	Fortune and you will never come together.
★★★	Enough to make you regret it.
★ ★ ★	That you have more sense than love.
★ ★ ★	Reply or leave it; it is immaterial.
★ ★ ★	The future for you is the colour of the rose, all beauty.
★ ★ ★	At the next snow storm.
★	An agreeable profession.
★★★★	A little agitation, but much peace.
★★ ★★	Never, nor a title.
★ ★ ★ ★	He believed it, he now believes it, and always will do so.
★ ★ ★ ★	It ought to make you feel it, but it will not.
★ ★ ★	It is nearer finished than you think.
★ ★★	One only, and she deceived him.
★ ★★ ★	Always, thanks to your audaciousness.

★ ★ ★	Foolish, wicked, and jealous.
★★	You will suffer, but grief will not kill you.
★ ★ ★	A secret confided to two, is no longer a secret.
★★★	That will depend upon your future conduct.
★ ★ ★	Credulity is a dangerous weakness.
★ ★ ★ ★	Nothing that will frighten you.
★ ★ ★ ★	Nobody thinks about it, because they know you wish it.
★ ★ ★	Your greatest enemy is yourself.
★	You will do better not to desire it.
★★★★	Live in the town if you like pleasure.
★★ ★★	Yes, above all after dinner.
★ ★ ★ ★	Leave him alone, and be silent.
★ ★ ★ ★	Their promises are as soon forgotten as made.
★ ★ ★ ★ ★	To the youngest, if you prefer fortune to love.
★ ★★ ★	No, he has loved before as well as you.
★ ★★ ★	Be wise by night as well as by day.

★ ★	Ugly, as it is to commit sin on Sunday.
★★	Do not be too hasty about it.
★ ★ ★	Much prettier than good.
★★★	He has always been so, and ever will be.
★ ★ ★	He has loved you more than he does now.
★ ★ ★	You could if you had it.
★ ★ ★	Much more than you think of him.
★ ★ ★ ★	Neither by night or by day.
★	They do not think it is worth their while to trouble about you.
★★★★	Your fear is without foundation.
★★ ★★	It will remain as it is, if you do not change.
★ ★ ★	You are a spoilt child; happiness and fortune both smile upon you.
★ ★ ★ ★	If you forgive once, it would be necessary to pardon you a thousand times.
★ ★ ★ ★ ★	If you receive them with one hand, give them away with the other.
★ ★★ ★	It is likely that he will never return.
★ ★★ ★	The one you will marry, will appear to you in a dream within three days.

★ ★	He ought to have enough for himself and you too.
★★	They are deceiving you, and it is your own fault.
★ ★ ★	That it is in accordance with your face.
★★★	You will be very foolish, if you let him suspect anything.
★ ★ ★	Yes, and he loves you with sincerity.
★ ★ ★	He was born before your father and mother.
★ ★ ★	They have reason enough to think so.
★ ★ ★	At night, after supper.
★	They do not think you very cruel.
★★★★	Repulse them with all your might.
★★ ★★	All advisers should be suspected.
★ ★ ★ ★	You will lose a great deal, but you will gain more.
★ ★ ★ ★	Not more so than your vows.
★ ★ ★ ★	They will be more productive than long.
★ ★★ ★	No, and it is well for you.
★ ★★ ★	Until to-morrow morning.

★ ★	You have had them, but they have now left you.
★★	You will be both happy and unhappy.
★ ★ ★	Yes, if you know how to merit forgiveness.
★★★	There is always time to yield, but it is often too late to break it off.
★ ★ ★	Be faithful to him, and do not complain.
★ ★ ★	Two, and the pair will be worth nothing.
★ ★ ★	He has an iron head, an icy hand, and leaden brains.
★ ★ ★	That is above your strength.
★	Only a few hours more.
★★★★	Much less evil than may otherwise occur.
★★ ★★	It is necessary to begin it again.
★ ★ ★ ★	He regrets not being with you.
★ ★ ★ ★	There is moderation in all things, even in frankness.
★ ★ ★ ★ ★	Nothing is wanting to make it both lasting and agreeable.
★ ★★ ★	It has already half diminished.
★ ★★ ★	It will cause you more pain than pleasure.

★ ★	You must be very foolish, if you believe them.
★★	You ought to do so always.
★ ★ ★	To cease to be so, you should be one now.
★★★	A charming one, and several detestable ones.
★ ★ ★	Are you not already married in jest.
★ ★ ★	Three at a time to begin with, that promises well.
★ ★ ★	Like in many other things, act in disguise.
★ ★ ★	Very little.
★	Sorrow generally follows a life devoted to pleasure.
★★★★	You will die a wife, but not a widow.
★★ ★★	Always, and very fondly.
★ ★ ★ ★	You envy others, more than you are envied.
★ ★ ★ ★	Obey your conscience.
★ ★ ★ ★	Yes, for your happiness.
★ ★★ ★	A lame messenger walks but slowly.
★ ★★ ★	His love goes on at the same rate as your own.

★ ★ ★	That depends upon your prudence.
★★	Rich in love, but poor in money.
★ ★ ★	There is an insurmountable obstacle to your marriage.
★★★	A moderate fortune, but honestly acquired.
★ ★ ★	Search after them if you like, but they will cause you grief.
★ ★ ★	He thinks that you could not be more amiable, but might be wiser.
★ ★ ★	To reply, would be to stretch forth your foot, and to take a false step.
★ ★ ★	From henceforth all ought to smile upon you.
★	When time shall have ripened your reason.
★★★★	His work will often keep him away from you.
★★ ★★	Frequent tempests and few calms.
★ ★ ★ ★	You have a rich relation, who often thinks of you.
★ ★ ★ ★	He does not believe much in women.
★ ★ ★ ★	They will be less disastrous than you think.
★ ★★ ★	Not soon, but it will terminate to your advantage.
★ ★★ ★	He has been wiser than you.

★ ★	Be more prudent than you are at present.
★★	Sweet-tempered, modest, easy to be persuaded.
★ ★ ★	Happy will he be who cures you of the illness which now threatens you.
★★★	It will not be discovered for a long time.
★ ★ ★	You may meet with any accident, but be wise, and act prudently.
★ ★ ★	Promises have wings and often fly away.
★ ★ ★	The first man which will pay his addresses to you, is still in leading strings.
★ ★ ★	He will try to do so but without success.
★	You never ought to have any.
★★★★	No, for you are insatiable.
★★ ★★	They both suit you, one as well as the other.
★ ★ ★	If you allow it, you will be lost.
★ ★ ★ ★	You will do better to attend to your household occupations.
★ ★ ★ ★	They could only keep the first.
★ ★★ ★	Two are not too many for you, keep them both.
★ ★★ ★	You are his first love, and will be his last.

★ ★ ★	Yes, one that you know very well.
★★	As ugly as you are pretty.
★ ★ ★ ★	Everything succeeds with those that have patience.
★★★	Your flatterers will say Yes, - but the Oracle says No.
★ ★ ★	He has been more so than he will ever be again.
★ ★ ★	He does not know himself.
★ ★ ★	How can you give that which you have not.
★ ★ ★	He is thinking of you, he dreams of you and, in fact, is madly in love.
★	Between the two.
★★★★	Yes, but do not say anything very good.
★★ ★★	It is founded, for the evil is done.
★ ★ ★ ★	You do not take care enough of it, for that.
★ ★ ★ ★	I only see that you are surrounded by pleasure.
★ ★ ★ ★	The forgiveness will have no good results.
★ ★★ ★	That will depend upon a whim.
★ ★★ ★	He is preparing to start on a journey.

★ ★	Long enough for the reconciliation to be charming.
★★	Just as much as you have.
★ ★ ★	You will be wrong if you doubt it.
★★★	That it would be better if it were less lively.
★ ★ ★	He will have suspicions, but never be certain.
★ ★ ★	Have you not already committed a thousand follies to win him.
★ ★ ★	As young as you, and not any wiser.
★ ★ ★	Yes, a spoilt child.
★	At every time, and in every place.
★★★★	That you are too lively.
★★ ★★	You may accept them, but not yet.
★ ★ ★ ★	Advisers are generally worthless.
★ ★ ★	You have lost all you had to lose.
★ ★ ★ ★	Sincerity is not for you.
★ ★★ ★	Yes, and you will soon begin them.
★ ★★ ★	He is not simpleton enough for that.

★ ★	It will be more pleasant than advantageous.
★★	You have none at present, but will soon be troubled by them.
★ ★ ★	There is as great a difference between love and happiness as paradise and hell.
★★★	You have no hope of forgiveness.
★ ★ ★	With a little management you may prevent both.
★ ★ ★	To suffer and be silent is the greatest virtue of a woman.
★ ★ ★	Several in jest, and one who will cause you to weep.
★ ★ ★	It is the most frank, the most honest, and loving heart that exists.
★	Do not be in too much hurry.
★★★★	For an entire year.
★★ ★★	That which has already happened.
★ ★ ★ ★	Very bad, if you are not very cautious.
★ ★ ★ ★	He suffers and is pining away, like a plant without the sun.
★ ★ ★ ★ ★	What is the use of it, when everybody knows it.
★ ★★ ★	Yes, if you are indulgent.
★ ★★ ★	It has lasted twice as long as it has to last.

★ ★	He would do so if......but......
★★	You know that they cannot be.
★ ★ ★	The first day only.
★★★	Oh! dear young lady, you make me laugh.
★ ★ ★	Yes, before and after.
★ ★ ★	In twelve years that will be talked about.
★ ★ ★	One for the day, another for the afternoon, and a third for the night.
★ ★ ★	To be loved, you must be amiable.
★	You ought to be eternally regretted.
★★★★	It will be troubled by repentance.
★★ ★★	You will have been a widow, but will be married again.
★ ★ ★ ★	The love that you inspire will have more power than duration.
★ ★ ★ ★	That ought not to prevent your sleeping.
★ ★ ★ ★	You ought to, but you will not do so.
★ ★★ ★	If it ought to have changed, it would have done so.
★ ★★ ★	Yes, if he does not get lost on the way.

★ ★	You are the first of the third series.
★★	You will sail against wind and tide.
★ ★ ★	Rich in money, but poor in intelligence.
★★★	Yes, if you wish to die of grief.
★ ★ ★	Much more than you deserve.
★ ★ ★ ★	Enough to make you know the world.
★ ★ ★	That it is very difficult for the learned to be amiable.
★ ★ ★	Yes, do it, or you will surely die.
★	Sorrow has fled away, not to return again.
★★★★	When you cease to feel for others.
★★ ★★	He will have two professions, one of which will be good.
★ ★ ★ ★	Very violently, but not for long.
★ ★ ★ ★	Yes, a very fine one, but the lawyers will eat the half for you.
★ ★ ★ ★	As good as the generality of women.
★ ★★ ★	You have committed the fault, and must bear the punishment.
★ ★★ ★	It is nearly concluded.

★ ★	He has loved a great many, but in a different way.
★★	You would have a great deal to do, as it must be discovered.
★ ★ ★	Careless but kind hearted.
★★★	You will be a charming imaginary invalid.
★ ★ ★	No, if you do not lose presence of mind.
★ ★ ★	Your home will be a veritable paradise.
★ ★ ★	That would be altogether foolish.
★ ★ ★	Nothing if you are strong, much if you are weak.
★	There is time enough yet.
★★★★	Yes, but you will soar above them all.
★★ ★★	It will be perfectly satisfied.
★ ★ ★ ★	In the town, if you would become rich.
★ ★ ★	It is by him that you will become rich.
★ ★ ★ ★	Do not meddle with what you do not understand.
★ ★★ ★	That will not be without difficulty.
★ ★★ ★ ★	To the first that shall cause you to weep.

★ ★	He does not think about returning, but thinks of marrying.
★★	A man that did not know you would not marry you.
★ ★ ★	He will be charming, but he will know too much.
★★★	The later the better.
★ ★ ★	Yes, at night, without light and without moon.
★ ★ ★	I cannot say much about that.
★ ★ ★	Alas, he is unfortunate, to do that.
★ ★ ★	You may do it without running much risk.
★	He thinks and sighs, but you will not let him suffer long.
★★★★	Nothing of the sort ought ever to arrive.
★★ ★★	They are relating your adventures.
★ ★ ★ ★	Yes, but there are remedies for all evils.
★ ★ ★ ★	You have already done all you could, to lose it.
★ ★ ★ ★	No, if you are prudent.
★ ★★ ★	Wait till they have merited pardon.
★ ★★ ★	You will do well not wait for them, and better not to receive them.

★ ★	He has told more stories than he will ever tell again.
★★	Until you take the first step towards the reconciliation.
★ ★ ★	Enough to make his fortune.
★★★	The results alone will prove that.
★ ★ ★	That you wish it to appear more than it is.
★ ★ ★	Husbands are always the last to suspect those who deceive them.
★ ★ ★	It knows it perfectly well, but it does not affect him.
★ ★ ★	He will be an old man.
★	They have showed you to the contrary several times.
★★★★	In the middle of the day.
★★ ★★	They think that you are not modest enough.
★ ★ ★ ★	Yes, but without conditions.
★ ★ ★	Neither the advice or the advisers are worth a pin.
★ ★ ★	You must know how to lose to learn how to gain.
★ ★★ ★	It is but another piece of folly.
★ ★★ ★	One only, which will be as much as many generally are.

★ ★	It is but a cloud which will soon disappear.
★★	It will cost you more tears than it will give you pleasure.
★ ★ ★	One only which is not dangerous.
★★★	Love has never been the road to happiness.
★ ★ ★	They will not forgive you.
★ ★ ★	Your heart should be your only guide.
★ ★ ★	Hide the past and do better for the future.
★ ★ ★	You will have too many, if you only have one.
★	His heart is affectionate, more's the pity, for you will deceive him.
★★★★	If you renounce it too soon, you will return to it again.
★★ ★★	Much longer than you would wish it to be.
★ ★ ★ ★	You know it by experience.
★ ★ ★ ★	It will not be brilliant enough for you.
★ ★ ★	He is dreaming of sweet futurity.
★ ★★ ★	You will gain nothing by denying the truth.
★ ★★ ★	Yes, if you become reasonable, which is very doubtful.

★ ★	You will have to wait as long as you have already waited.
★★	Very so, and it is right that he should.
★ ★ ★	As sincere as it is possible to be.
★★★	As happy, as you were before unhappy.
★ ★ ★	You will do as your mother did before you.
★ ★ ★	It would be better for you, not to have any.
★ ★ ★	You should never marry.
★ ★ ★	You will be continually changing.
★	You would perform miracles without succeeding in gaining his love.
★★★★	Tears and regret are reserved for you.
★★ ★★	If you make a hard bed, you must lie on it.
★ ★ ★ ★	You will die of a good old age, and will be a widow.
★ ★ ★ ★	Very little, and very faintly.
★ ★ ★ ★	Yes, and they are apparently your best friends.
★ ★★ ★	You will never do it too soon.
★ ★★ ★	Never, it is your destiny.

★ ★	No, it is impossible.
★★	No one marries the first woman he loves.
★ ★ ★	Yes, even in spite of your follies.
★★★	If he is not rich at present, he soon will be.
★ ★ ★	Do not hope it is impossible.
★ ★ ★	Yes, if you conduct yourself prudently.
★ ★ ★	You will have more than one, which you will not be able to boast of.
★ ★ ★	He thinks well of you, but he will soon change his mind.
★	If things go on so fast they will not last long.
★★★★	Great joy and very little sorrow.
★★ ★★	When your heart ceases to beat.
★ ★ ★ ★	He will never need to get his living.
★ ★ ★ ★	Peaceful, troubled but by few storms.
★ ★ ★ ★	You will inherit.......debts.
★ ★★	His powers of believing do not reach that point.
★ ★★ ★	No one escapes the necessary consequence of their conduct.

★ ★	To the one that you see first.
★★	First love is always the strongest.
★ ★ ★	It is impossible to hide those things a long time.
★★★	Lively, gay, but obliging and good.
★ ★ ★	You will always have Joy, Health, and Prosperity.
★ ★ ★	It is already discovered.
★ ★ ★	Household affairs will give you a foretaste of hell.
★ ★ ★	They wish to deceive you and will succeed.
★	The same that happened to Eve for eating the forbidden fruit.
★★★★	One thinks about it, and only needs a word of encouragement to begin.
★★ ★★	Yes, but they fear you.
★ ★ ★ ★	Yes, if you take care to be cautious.
★ ★ ★ ★	In the country, if you are wise.
★ ★ ★	It will be a source of much happiness.
★ ★★ ★	Yes, but with much management.
★ ★★ ★	They are already thinking of disengaging themselves from them.

★ ★	You will have to wait a long time for them.
★★	He is too well off where he is to wish to leave it.
★ ★ ★	How should you know him, when he is not born.
★★★	Love will embellish him with a thousand charms.
★ ★ ★	Ask the advice of others.
★ ★ ★	Opinions on that subject are divided.
★ ★ ★	Yes.
★ ★ ★ ★	He adores you, and suffers, but he will take his revenge.
★	Yes, if you like pleasure more than honour.
★★★★	As they would think of a little person of no importance.
★★ ★★	A little before sunrise.
★ ★ ★ ★	They are making fun of you.
★ ★ ★ ★	It would be better for you, if it were.
★ ★ ★ ★	It is a fragile jewel, that you knock too hard.
★ ★★ ★	Real sorrow should be always unseen by others.
★ ★★ ★	Forgive now, or never.

⁙ (two stars stacked)	Long and short, and very often.
★★	His veracity is equal to yours.
★ ★ ★ (stacked)	It ought to be eternal.
★★★	He has a little but it will last a long time.
★ ★ ★ (stacked)	The more you give the less they will return you.
★ ★ ★ (stacked)	That it is rusting for want of using.
★ / ★ ★	No, his eyes will be shut by love.
★ ★ / ★	Whether he knows it or not, you should renounce him.
★	The youngest are not always the best, so much the worse for you.
★★★★	Yes, but a child that would willingly be thought a woman.
★★ / ★★	A little after midnight.
★ / ★ / ★ ★	They do not, that you are as good as you really are.
★ ★ / ★	Yes, in changing some part of them.
★ / ★ ★ / ★	You are strong enough to fly with your own wings.
★ / ★★ / ★	Loss of money is not what you have most to dread.
★ / ★★ / ★	It is but a new snare, to entrap you.

★ ★	Enough to cause you deep regret.
★★	It is you alone that can make it cease.
★ ★ ★	It will be the cause of your first happiness.
★★★	You are surrounded by them at this minute.
★ ★ ★	To be happy in love, you must give way to the wishes of others.
★ ★ ★	Those who repent are easily forgiven.
★ ★ ★	There is as much danger on one side as on the other.
★ ★ ★	Be always the same.
★	One for the day and another for night.
★★★★	Affectionate is not the word, it should be soft.
★★ ★★	You have not strength of mind enough for that.
★ ★ ★ ★	For a long time it has not been free.
★ ★ ★ ★	That regret will follow pleasure.
★ ★ ★ ★	More agreeable than productive.
★ ★★ ★	He is making grand projects, that he will relinquish to-morrow.
★ ★★ ★	Choose a favourable instant for that.

★ ★	It is now, as it always should be.
★★	Better for you to be without it.
★ ★ ★	The honeymoon cannot always last.
★★★	It was but a touch stone to try your self-esteem.
★ ★ ★	As long as you will merit it.
★ ★ ★ ★	You will never cease to be one.
★ ★ ★	Every year, and handsome like their father.
★ ★ ★	When the first wrinkles shall appear on your forehead.
★	You will have them of all sizes, colours, and tempers.
★★★★	I advise you not to undertake impossibilities.
★★ ★★	They will mourn after you, for a long time.
★ ★ ★	Yes, if you know how to keep a pear against you if you're thirsty.
★ ★ ★ ★	You will die before your fourth husband.
★ ★ ★ ★	Much longer than necessary.
★ ★★ ★	Act as though they were not, and you will soon find that there are plenty.
★ ★★ ★	Yes, and you will not repent it.

★ ★ ★	It will have the most natural consequences.
★★	Sooner than it could have been expected.
★ ★ ★ ★	Yes, the first he has seriously loved.
★★★	Success and reverse will be your lot.
★ ★ ★	Riches will be his only good quality.
★ ★ ★	Without a minister you may.
★ ★ ★	Fortune will come to you, while you are sleeping.
★ ★ ★	It appears that the first has given you a liking for them.
★	That you are beautiful, good, gracious, and charming.
★★★★	Yes, if you wish to reply to stories.
★★ ★★	There will be a perfect compensation.
★ ★ ★ ★	You could never renounce so sweet a thing.
★ ★ ★ ★	He will use the file or the plane.
★ ★ ★ ★	You will not taste much repose.
★ ★★ ★	Yes, it will come slowly.
★ ★★ ★	He is not ignorant of any of your actions.

★ ★	Like promises are never kept.
★★	To the one who waits the longest.
★ ★ ★	Never, but he yet may.
★★★	Change of conduct and of country.
★ ★ ★	He will be a churlish dog.
★ ★ ★	Yes, it will be your only happiness.
★ ★ ★	If it is not now, it never will be.
★ ★ ★	He will think more about himself, than about you.
★	Take care not to be led away by them.
★★★★	You will gather sweet fruit, which will soon become bitter.
★★ ★★	As you now wish it, so will you soon regret it.
★ ★ ★	Of all colours and all sizes.
★ ★ ★ ★	No, not if you do not lose your self-possession.
★ ★ ★ ★	In the country if you can brave *l'ennui.*
★ ★★ ★	Do not refuse but remember reason.
★ ★★ ★	You will do better to leave him alone.

★ ★	Forgive, if you would be forgiven.
★★	Do not reckon upon it, it will be a false joy.
★ ★ ★	He will return by Easter or Trinity Sunday.
★★★	You will go from a known to an unknown one.
★ ★ ★	Too handsome to be faithful to you.
★ ★ ★	No, renounce it immediately.
★ ★ ★	They are obliged to, as you are exceedingly pretty.
★ ★ ★	He loves you too much to think of another.
★	He loves you as you deserve to be loved.
★★★★	Take care, he is more artful than he appears to be.
★★ ★★	Not now, but he will if you give him encouragement.
★ ★ ★	By the light of the moon.
★ ★ ★ ★	They are discussing your merit.
★ ★ ★	You have less than ever to fear.
★ ★★ ★	Yes, but some pretended friend, will try to calumniate you.
★ ★★ ★	Walk uprightly, and fear nothing.

★ ★	It is but to trifle with you.
★★	You do not need them, to make you perfect.
★ ★ ★	He only tells you the truth when he forgets himself.
★★★	It would last for ever if you were wise.
★ ★ ★	A little, perhaps.
★ ★ ★	You know that it is impossible.
★ ★ ★	That you are very deficient of this article.
★ ★ ★	He will be more jealous than loving.
★	Yes, but he knows that your love is divided with others.
★★★★	Yes, but that will be his only merit.
★★ ★★	You will be always thought one for your wisdom.
★ ★ ★	In silence and darkness.
★ ★ ★	You are thought to have had more than one adventure.
★ ★ ★	Only accept them conditionally.
★ ★★ ★	This is the advice that lost Eve and the whole human race.
★ ★★ ★	No, if you act with prudence and loyalty.

★ ★	Whatever you do, do not be in a hurry.
★★	It cannot and ought not to be.
★ ★ ★	Its duration will be proportioned to its depth.
★★★	It will afford you Joy, Health, and Prosperity.
★ ★ ★	Several, but you will soar above them all.
★ ★ ★	No doubt of it, for love is your element.
★ ★ ★	They know all, and forgive you.
★ ★ ★	Never mind the dispute, a reconciliation will be sure to follow.
★	Do not appear agitated when in his company.
★★★★	One that you will govern, and one that will govern you.
★★ ★★	Yes, and his heart beats but for you.
★ ★ ★	The sooner the better.
★ ★ ★ ★	It will no longer be yours in eight days.
★ ★ ★	That you will neither be richer or poorer by it.
★ ★★ ★	More productive than agreeable.
★ ★★ ★	He is acting foolishly.

★ ★	Yes, if you wish to be quickly reconciled.
★★	It will change for the better but very slowly.
★ ★ ★	You will yet count many more months and weeks.
★★★	His love is less lively, but more lasting.
★ ★ ★	Truth has never been spoken, by the mouth that uttered them.
★ ★ ★	Yes, if you succeed in correcting yourself.
★ ★ ★	That entirely depends upon yourself.
★ ★ ★	Several but they will not at all resemble their father.
★	What difference will that make to you.
★★★★	Try to persuade yourself that quality is preferable to quantity.
★★ ★★	Do not trouble yourself about him, he is already engaged.
★ ★ ★	That will depend on how you act.
★ ★ ★ ★	Yes, if you act honestly and uprightly.
★ ★ ★ ★	An old maid, but rich.
★ ★★ ★	It would be impossible to love you long.
★ ★★ ★	Fools indeed would those be that could envy you.

★ ★	He must be a simpleton to think so.
★★	No, if you do not begin again.
★ ★ ★	If it terminates to your advantage, it has already terminated.
★★★	He had only loved a few dozens.
★ ★ ★	Yes, if you do not discourage him.
★ ★ ★	Rich, Miserly, Jealous, and Slovenly.
★ ★ ★	Neither him or any other.
★ ★ ★	A very large one, but you must wait for it.
★	Yes, you will walk over an adventurous path, but it will not be strewed with roses.
★★★★	That you are the only woman that could make him happy.
★★ ★★	Wait at least for the second.
★ ★ ★	As much of one as of the other.
★ ★ ★	When the stars dance at midnight.
★ ★ ★	He will be a tradesman.
★ ★★ ★	Folly is the enemy of repose.
★ ★★ ★	Yes, a very large one, and that very soon.

★ ★	Yes, if you wish to ruin him.
★★	They promise, but never perform.
★ ★ ★	To the one who talks least, and acts most.
★★★	As much, Yes, ...More, No.
★ ★ ★	Avoid the world, and repent.
★ ★ ★ ★	He will be a grumbling, brutal, and sullen fellow.
★ ★ ★	Yes, if you do not spoil it.
★ ★ ★	When it is, there will be no more danger for you.
★	Yes, if love will suffice for you.
★★★★	That would be the greatest folly that you could be capable of.
★★ ★★	That you will be cured of your mad passion.
★ ★ ★ ★	Yes, but it will not last long, though it will cost you a great deal.
★ ★ ★ ★	Yes, some very powerful ones.
★ ★ ★ ★	Yes, but not for a long time.
★ ★★ ★	In the town, if you are more than fifteen years of age.
★ ★★ ★	Have you not been put to trial.

★ ★	To suffer, and to enjoy is to live.
★★	You have no right to be severe.
★ ★ ★	They are preparing them to offer you.
★★★	He is going farther off, instead of returning.
★ ★ ★	You know him better than he knows you.
★ ★ ☆	As ugly physically as morally.
★ ★ ★	You never conceived a better one.
★ ★ ★	Men say, Yes; Women say, No.
★	Fidelity is a virtue that he possesses as much as you.
★★★★	He once loved you, but his love is passing away.
★★ ★★	Do not be hasty, there is always time to give.
★ ★ ★	He would think of you, if he knew how to be loved.
★ ★ ★ ★	At sunrise.
★ ★ ★ ★	Yes they are talking well of you.
★ ★★	Be careful to be on your guard.
★ ★★ ★	It will always be as you make it.

★ ★	It is not your purse that they want.
★★	Yes, perfectly sincere.
★ ★ ★	Yes, if you are not wise enough to dispense with them.
★★★	For every lie you tell him, he tells two.
★ ★ ★	Still two days and three long nights.
★ ★ ★	Yes, it shows itself in his eyes.
★ ★ ★	You have been, but you will no longer be.
★ ★ ★	What can they think, when they know you are without any.
★	Yes, but if you are frank, he will forgive the past.
★★★★	Yes, and it makes him the happiest of men.
★★ ★★	He will be but a school boy, but will be your master.
★ ★ ★ ★ ★	Yes, and a terrible child.
★ ★ ★ ★ ★	At midday, before witnesses.
★ ★ ★ ★ ★	They think you more amiable than you are.
★ ★★ ★	Do not accept the smallest part of them.
★ ★★ ★	You will lose nothing by following them.

★ ★	He is not thinking about you, but of another.
★★	If you avow that, you will have to avow a great deal more.
★ ★ ★	It will not last as long as it has lasted.
★★★	They are thinking how they can relieve you from it.
★ ★ ★	Yes, if it is made in the day. No, if it is made in the night.
★ ★ ★	Two, one of which will dethrone you.
★ ★ ★	That will depend upon your conduct.
★ ★ ★	There are some faults which can never be forgiven.
★	If he loves you, the dispute is not to be feared.
★★★★	Abstain from certain habits that displease him.
★★ ★★	A tall one, a short one, a middle sized, and not one too many.
★ ★ ★ ★	Never were two hearts better formed for each other.
★ ★ ★ ★	Yes, if you wish to live long.
★ ★ ★ ★	You are too giddy for that.
★ ★★ ★	The more you give, the more you will receive.
★ ★★ ★	All your foresight will be of no avail.

★ ★	What, do you wish them to envy you?
★★	Certainly, as you are wrong.
★ ★ ★	It is very near changing, so much the worse for you.
★★★	It comes slowly, but it will arrive at last.
★ ★ ★	Men never love their wives as they loved their sweethearts.
★ ★ ★ ★	They were telling stories, and you knew it well.
★ ★ ★	As long as you love sincerely.
★ ★ ★	Yes, but no one will know it.
★	It will not be your fault, if you have none.
★★★★	You will wish to be thought young, but will be old.
★★ ★★	Three that will cause you pleasure, and ten that will cause you grief.
★ ★ ★ ★	If you could work wonders, it would be of no use.
★ ★ ★	No, if you rest as you are.
★ ★ ★ ★	Remembrances will make it happy.
★ ★★ ★	You will die maid or widow.
★ ★★ ★	Yes, if you are faithful.

★ ★	Those who wait for dead people's shoes, often go barefoot a long time.
★★	He has known a long time what to believe.
★ ★ ★	You are wrong to dread them, as they will be agreeable.
★★★	The longer it lasts, the better it will be for you.
★ ★ ★	He had as many ladies as you had lovers.
★ ★	You will lose at first, but will afterwards gain.
★ ★ ★	He will be rich in good qualities.
★ ★ ★	You may ask me the same question in ten years.
★	It would be hoping in vain.
★★★★	You will have many.
★★ ★★	Neither good or bad; he looks and waits.
★ ★ ★	You are in a great hurry, then, to deceive him.
★ ★ ★	Joy will surpass sorrow.
★ ★ ★	When it is daylight at midnight.
★ ★★ ★	He will do nothing of any consequence.
★ ★★ ★	Much more peaceful than you wish it to be.

★ ★	Always and everywhere.
★★	Do not meddle with what does not concern you.
★ ★ ★	They were as soon forgotten as made.
★★★	To one that appears the least interested at first.
★ ★ ★	Not as much, but much more.
★ ★ ★	Be more discreet than you are at present.
★ ★ ★	Benevolent, credulous, and resigned.
★ ★ ★	Do not sacrifice yourself to pleasure.
★	Yes, as you have confided it to an indiscreet person.
★★★★	Happiness is not for you.
★★ ★★	Yes, for they are sincere.
★ ★ ★	That you will be laughed at and despised.
★ ★ ★ ★	Do not be in such a hurry to play with the fire.
★ ★ ★ ★	Yes, but they can do no mischief.
★ ★★ ★	Much sooner than you hope.
★ ★★ ★	In the country, if you have renounced love.

* * *	It never has been good.
**	Yes, but it will be followed with much joy.
* * *	You have already waited too long.
***	Yes, but you will pay dearly for them.
* * *	He will return as soon as possible.
* * *	You have known him a long time.
* * *	He will be in every way charming.
* * *	Consult your friends, and act prudently.
*	Yes, when you do not show your two faces.
****	He wishes to, but cannot.
** **	He has passed the gradation, a little........very much......passionately......not at all.
* * *	Yes, it will only make one more.
* * *	When he sees you, and that is all.
* * *	Early in the morning.
* ** *	They do not even think of you.
* ** *	It has never had the least foundation.

★ ★	Examine and reason a little first.
★★	It is not money that you would lose.
★ ★ ★	Deceiver, it is well for you to exact sincerity.
★★★	Very long and very productive ones.
★ ★ ★	For every two lies you tell him, he tells you three.
★ ★ ★	It will finish as soon as you like.
★ ★ ★	Too much, to love you long.
★ ★ ★	Not yet, but you will be.
★	That you would do better to have no pretensions to it.
★★★★	He cannot help having suspicions.
★★ ★★	He has thought so, but dared not hope for so much happiness.
★ ★ ★ ★	He was born in the same year as you.
★ ★ ★ ★	They know that there are no children in this age.
★ ★ ★	In the middle of some dark night.
★ ★★ ★	They have an excellent opinion of it.
★ ★★ ★	Accept them by all means.

★ ★ ★	Less gratifying than you had hoped.
★★	He is thinking of your last interview.
★ ★ ★	If you confess it, you are lost.
★★★	Bad acquaintances are generally kept the longest.
★ ★ ★	Some friend is preparing consolation for you.
★ ★ ★	You will gain nothing by it.
★ ★ ★	One that will cause you much grief.
★ ★ ★	For that it would be necessary to have what you have not.
★	You will be pardoned, but they will keep you in suspense.
★★★★	Neither one nor the other.
★★ ★★	Be more amiable in the *tete-a-tete*.
★ ★ ★	As many as you wish for, but you will be better without them.
★ ★ ★	Why should that concern you, as he will never be anything to you.
★ ★ ★	The world is poisoning you.
★ ★★ ★	It would be better for you if it did.
★ ★★ ★	Do not give away what you can sell.

★ ★	Always, but not always as much as at present.
★★	Those that you have are not dangerous.
★ ★ ★	You are in a great hurry to humiliate yourself.
★★★	Yes, and you will regret it for a long time.
★ ★ ★	You will receive them too soon for your own good.
★ ★ ★	Love is dying away, and friendship is taking its place.
★ ★ ★	You may believe them.
★ ★ ★	As long as you know how to hide your game.
★	No, thanks to chance.
★★★★	Before, yes.....after, no.
★★ ★★	You will be younger than wise.
★ ★ ★ ★	One only that will give you more happiness than a hundred.
★ ★ ★ ★	Show yourself as you are.
★ ★ ★ ★	A little, not much.
★ ★★ ★	It will be very different from your youth.
★ ★★ ★ ★	Widow and rich.

★ ★ ★	There ought to be no peace for you.
★★	It would be folly to hope it.
★ ★ ★ ★	He believes you to be as good as most others.
★★★	Yes, but they will pass like other things.
★ ★ ★	It will last longer than it has lasted.
★ ★ ★	Before he knew you he only changed ladies once a month.
★ ★ ★	You have not perseverance enough for that.
★ ★ ★	Do not look for happiness in riches.
★	If you marry him to-day, you will weep to-morrow.
★★★★	You will possess a fortune, but will not know how to keep it.
★★ ★★	A few, early in the morning.
★ ★ ★ ★	That you amuse yourself by teasing him.
★ ★ ★	You will be lost if you do so.
★ ★ ★ ★	Your greatest sorrows are past.
★ ★★ ★	When cats have eyes in their tails like peacocks.
★★ ★	He will wear a sword or a long robe.

★ ★	Stay where you are.
★★	Yes, by night as well as by day.
★ ★ ★	Yes, if you are tired of being happy.
★★★	They will keep them all, and will even do more.
★ ★ ★	The choice is easy, one is no better than the other.
★ ★ ★	Not one, but many.
★ ★ ★	Be reserved, and do not begin again.
★ ★ ★	As good as yours is bad.
★	That will depend upon your conduct.
★★★★	Yes, sooner or later, take care of yourself.
★★ ★★	You ought never to know sorrow.
★ ★ ★ ★	You may believe it without danger, if they do not exact more.
★ ★ ★	You know well what generally happens under similar circumstances.
★ ★ ★ ★	Not for several years.
★ ★★ ★	None to be really feared.
★ ★★ ★	It will be your own fault if it is not.

★ ★	Yes, it has good foundation.
★★	The truth will soon be known.
★ ★ ★	You will have more pleasure than sorrow.
★★★	Have you not also need of forgiveness.
★ ★ ★	Yes, if you are not wise enough to refuse them.
★ ★ ★	The later the better.
★ ★ ★	Only two days ago you spoke to him.
★ ★ ★	He will be as beautiful as a demon.
★	It is either too soon or too late; wait a little.
★★★★	Prettier than amiable, and more coquettish than pretty.
★★ ★★	He is faithful to pleasure, for he indulges in it wherever he finds it.
★ ★ ★ ★	Much, too much, for he is fretting, and you laugh at him.
★ ★ ★ ★	You have granted it to many others, why not to him.
★ ★ ★ ★	Yes, and you will soon have a proof of it.
★ ★★ ★	At the crowing of the cock.
★ ★★ ★	Yes, much more than they ought to.

★ ★	Accept them, if you have nothing to lose.
★★	If you follow them, your ruin is certain.
★ ★ ★	If you know how to give up, you will lose nothing.
★★★	Vows and repentances are frequently but lies.
★ ★ ★	You will do well not to voyage farther than round your own room.
★ ★ ★	He takes care not to do that.
★ ★ ★	If it does not finish to-day, it will to-morrow.
★ ★ ★	Enough not to take chalk for cheese.
★	They render you fifty for a hundred.
★★★★	They do not talk or think about it.
★★ ★★	Do not be too sure; he may do so.
★ ★ ★ ★	Yes, but he does not think that it will last long.
★ ★ ★ ★	He will commit many follies to pretend he is.
★ ★ ★ ★	Yes, for a child which has teeth, and wishes but to bite every body.
★ ★★ ★	In the morning of some fine day.
★ ★★ ★	You are thought to be happier than you really are.

TO SEE A FUTURE HUSBAND

THE APPLE AND THE
LOOKING GLASS

Take a candle, and go alone to the looking glass; eat an apple before it; and some say you should comb your hair all the time; the face of your future husband will be seen in the glass, as if peeping over your shoulder.

Other Copper Beech Gift Books include:

Etiquette for Gentlemen

Rules for 'perfect behaviour' for the gentleman in every
woman's life.

Mangles Mops & Feather Brushes

Advice for the laundry and cleaning the old-fashioned
way.

How To Entertain Your Guests

A book of traditional indoor games originally collected
in 1911.

The Duties of Servants

A look at the above and below stairs life 100 years ago.

Other Copper Beech Gift Books include:

Poetry Thoughts & Merry Jests
Words of friendship from Victorian and Edwardian
Autograph Albums.

Love is like a Mutton Chop...
Wry words of love, 1840-1940

Hand-me-down Wisdom
A book of treasured words
'The threads of wisdom bind us all, generation to
generation, they are written in autograph books, passed
down in classrooms, kitchens, on chance meetings and in
so many other ways...'

Chains of Wisdom
More hand-me-down wisdom collected from people in
the public eye.

For your free catalogue write to
Copper Beech Publishing Ltd
P O Box 159, East Grinstead, Sussex RH19 4FS England